Where the Wilderness Lay Untamed

Brian Dennis Hartford

Original Poems by: Brian Dennis Hartford © 2023
Original Cover Art by: Brian Dennis Hartford © 2023
H. publications *is Registered Self-Publishing Trademark of Brain Dennis Hartford*

All rights reserved. No part of this book may be reproduced in any form or by any means without the prior written consent of the author, with the sole exception for brief quotes used in reviews of book. The right to litigation will be fully exercised in any or all cases involving intellectual or graphic design property theft or misuse of author's original intent.

Warning: These poems may contain adult content, sexually graphic material, and some violence.

ISBN: 979-8-9857314-4-6
First Printing: December 2023

10 9 8 7 6 5 4 3 2 1

Printed in the United States of America

Introduction

Freedom awaits any who dares. Just know that freedom isn't always a heavenly place.

To a love shone truthful in the light of a trashcan fire.

CONTENTS

WHEN THE MARROW RUNS DRY	1
THE BEAUIFUL UGLY TRUTH	3
IN THE EMBERS OF ANGOLA	5
AND THE BOMBS WILL FALL REGARDLESS OF ANY LOVE	7
THE STATUE	9
BELOW, UPON THE KNOT	11
DEATH MACHINE	13
UPON THE ALTER WILD	17
HEADLIGHTS	19
IN THE ANNUM OF OUR MOMENT	21
PARIS, 3AM	23
IN THE DAWNING OF LILITH	25
EVAPORATION	27
AMIDST SNOWFLAKES STILL HOPEFUL	29
VIRGA	31
WHAT IS ART? THE ARTIST	33
WRITE ME	35
CHEAP GIN & CIGARETTES	37
THE HUSTLE	39
BAREFOOT UPON IMMORTAL LEAVES	41
THE STORM AMIDST A SUNNY DAY	43
MAYBE NEXT TIME	45

HOW HEAVY IS THE PEN	47
THE GARDENER'S RAKE	49
"WILLST SIE NOCH EINE ZIGARETTE?"	51
MAYBE…(IN ANOTHER DRINK OR TWO)	53
BRICK BY BRICK…	55
FALL IN BERLIN	57
UNTIL THE NEXT *"Hello"*	59
MY ЯYꟼMAV	61
WE'LL KNOW THE OTHER IN THE END	63
ONE LAST CHANCE, BUT IT AIN'T ANYWHERE 'ROUND HERE	65
WHERE THE WILDERNESS LAY UNTAMED	67

WHEN THE MARROW RUNS DRY

Somewhere, is a last call upon the stage

Where the marrow had long run dry

Thirsting of a last drop

For when words came from the pen so clear

And the heart knew their pace

What was that taste

Of when I had a voice

A page reveling in that one defining line

Found in perfect poetic end

And before a million faces

I stood, the messiah

Mouthing words poetic and poison

A mortal's mourning for the undead

What was that taste

Of when I had a voice

A page reveling in those defining lines

Found in perfect ends

And under the lone light

Upon the barren stage

Before empty seats

I'll face the final call

And know the moment when the marrow runs dry in the bone.

THE BEAUIFUL UGLY TRUTH

Her hands were soft in his

A touch not unlike the rays of the morning sun

Yet firm in the simple truth

That love is a dangerous thing.

And upon the red tiled shower floor

Where the blood washes down

Still lay hope

Cut up piece by piece

And cast way to the tides

Down into the depths where revenge waits impatient and ever hungry.

And her hands were soft in his

Where the morning sun warmed their bodies

Upon the alter above the sea

Where below, her soul awaited

And they fell fast to sleep, content in the beautiful ugly truth.

IN THE EMBERS OF ANGOLA

It was in the embers drifting upwards in the rancid smoke, reflected as red stars in her eyes that I found my love in the new Africa

Beyond, just inside some forgotten colonial place, punk bands rage with all the ferocity and angst of the Sex Pistols, Black Flag, or TSOL, but with one hundred times the truth to life no son or daughter of the west might ever know.

And outside, by the glow of a trash can barrel fire, she smiles
Furtive in the passing of Three Ships
Hips sway to the instruments of the coming destruction
Ignoring of what the fire-sparks cracking still warn
Choosing a moment instead, a first kiss over western bull-whip policy

And in her room, we love
Sweat in the humid night
The taste of salt upon our tongues
For water is precious no matter the form here

And there is no color to survival
But the grey of coming anarchy.

AND THE BOMBS WILL FALL REGARDLESS OF ANY LOVE

I knew defiance in the taste of sweat upon gun-powdered skin
Above where the bombs fell
In the place where our hearts would part
When a rifle had become her first love.

I knew the fire of the rubble reflected upon grey eyes
Out on the street where her home lay burning
Broken bricks upon street-side garden flowers
And her box of long kept love letters blowing way.

And I still know that last kiss upon quietly determined rough and blistered lips
Of calloused hands slipping away from mine
Of a red Carnation tucked into the pocket of her field coat
For when, perhaps, there might be another better time for us.

And the bombs will fall
Regardless of any love.

THE STATUE

Have I kept you bound through all these years?

My silent statue upon the alter

To whom I once prayed

Recanting echoes of the verse, I still cannot escape

Far behind the iron ivied gate

Beyond in the dark wood

Where you, motionless, await resurrection.

And there in our wild wood

Far from a common place

Where the sun had placed you just right

The chisel makes its final mark

A fragile chain impervious to any escape

Forever binding of any hope

Immortal to any length of wait.

Does the sun still stream down through the leafy oak,

To break its light upon your pallid skin?

Enough perhaps, to reflect the sin

Where in each crack lay a lie

Hairline fishers that only faith might hope burnish away

By still faithful hands working to resurrect a soul where there was none

Deaf to the lullaby murmur of a sacrificial heart tumbling over stone in the black stream below.

Have I kept you bound through all these years?

Hands caught within a fragile chain

Feet held fast to the alter

A body well-formed but motionless and unable

For redemption requires a willing and an unbound heart

And lips upon which to ask of it

And thus, the hammer and chisel still lay idle to your desire of me.

BELOW, UPON THE KNOT

Her fingers pass upon the rope

A bitter end winding

Bound underhand

The bridle slipping tight upon the skin

Box Tie knots coiling, silken

Like the Python closing in upon a last breath

Let it slip

Let it slip

Let it slip

Down into the place

Where our souls found life beneath the knot

And love might yet leave us breathless…

Just enough.

DEATH MACHINE

From out upon the barren plain it came
As if born of ambition alone
The only warning; its trailing ambilocal cord of dust rising fast into the sky
Like smoke of a great fire but more fearful
For dust is the leaving of the earth from itself in death
And below the ominous foretelling cloud, an unearthly howl announcing its intention to feast.
I saw the dark spot growing
Like some hideous reverse sunrise
A bloodied red and brown sky blotting out the last good thing, blue, stars, the sun and moon
As it howls onwards, rushing
It's bones and flesh clank and rumble
Ravenous.
And there, upon the great beast rides the reapers
The final horseman
With eyes set only to oblivion
While below their stead glides steady onwards
Clanking and rumbling

Steel rolling out upon steel

An intercourse, maybe

The sound of cuming deeply

The announcement of a dark conception.

And terrified, we ran

But it was already too late

For the great feast was already upon us

Boxed and herded into the kill zone of concrete and convenience

The sound of the machine upon its rail deafening, driving relentlessly

The dead covered over in its passing

Foundations for yet more future, they had told us.

———————

And it was they, whom had found it,

The last born,

Far beyond the wasteland where no other dares to go

The great machine beast

Bloated and asleep amidst the ruin of a strange place long unknown for a millennium to any now.

They had felt it purring low and gentle inside

The cold of its bones and flesh

The smooth of its feet

A heat within still wanting

And upon its head was a strange device

Two stones, one red, and one green...

And fate had finally found the world as before Eden again.

UPON THE ALTER WILD

The tip of my tongue glides

Finding its way

Up one side

Then down another

Purposeful

As if a knife upon the skin

Seeking of that perfect place to strike

Below, down in-between

Where need lies

Expectant

As the stone wets

Beyond in the dark wood

At the edge of unknown temple steps

Where our kiss was the incantation

Calling up things deep and dangerous

Amidst the moonlit fern

Immersed in star reflecting waters

We swim bold within the black mirror

Watch our naked image fade way in concentric rippling rings

For reason had long given way to lust

To the taste, of us
To that sacred place, where
Once upon the alter, wild
We fucked.

HEADLIGHTS

Out on the lookout

The world seemed ours

Side by side

Arms crossed and looking up to the stars

Making wishes when they fall

Maybe that is our big mistake;

Wishes made upon dying things.

And we lean in for another kiss

Champaign fresh upon our lips

Lovers in the headlights of passing cars

Shakespearian silhouettes in play upon the asphalt stage

A besties photo beneath a streetlight green

Of hands upon the others face

The image of a thousand likes soon to be snapped way

Because news feeds too, are dying things.

And within the headlights of passing cars

We had found the traffic of our hearts

And cast our wishes there too, upon each

Passing fast one-by-one

Each a dying thing in its own right, headlights

For any key will soon kill that wish also.

IN THE ANNUM OF OUR MOMENT

The words run dry

A pen lay idle

The inkwell empty

A brush finds its way

But the colors all blend to black

As slumped as the clay upon the wheel

Ever turning

But without resolution

Hands and mind unable

The moment still running…

And in my darkest moments

It's still just us

Drifting and lost

Moments never seized

Moments turned to dust

Unwritten

The image gone unknown

In a sentence that might cause hope

In a painting that might cause love

In a sculpture of what was in our grandest moment...

And my voice runs dry in the image

Unable in the annum of our time

To speak in any way of me, or you, or what could have been

Us…

PARIS, 3AM

Paris, 3AM

Arm in arm along the Seine

Lost beneath the city lights

No money left for a taxi

Laughing anyways

Playing "splash" in rain puddled sidewalks

Two umbrellas lost on a train

Where might they go?

Begins the guessing game

Completing the other's sentence

Two strangers speaking as one

She wears his coat

His fingers place wet hair over her ear

Her head tilts

A gold pendant necklace plunges

Her lips hold back her tongue

In the feel of his lips upon hers

Hands upon his chest pushing slightly

Against that inevitable Paris moment

When the sounds of a city are drowned to the wanting of the heart

To the vision of two naked bodies under an antique mirrored ceiling

Clothes strewn upon the marble floor

Their motion set as if in a film

Caught focused in off-set lighting

Streaming through curtains half drawn

A window ajar

Cut to the sun rising

And the death of streetlights

Left to dream of night again.

And somewhere on a train in Paris;

"Might this be your umbrella?"

Her eyes meet his

Two strangers lost and laughing in the guessing games of;

"From where might they have come, or been?"

IN THE DAWNING OF LILITH

His hands probe upon her skin

As her eyes opened

Rough and uncaring

The circuitry within redirects from its systems check

Grasping at her breasts

Her Violet glass irises dilate from the strange light above

A mouth sucks

Where once there was only blackness

His phallic probes indiscriminate

To now a sun

He gasps...

And within her womb

Lay gods' grand deception.

EVAPORATION

Drop by drop

The sweat of us lifts upwards

Slowly turned to little more than a nightly haunting from my skin

Sort of what the rain must feel like falling upon desert sands

A momentary hopefulness

Cut short in the chance to begin

Lost to that moment between what was

And what might have been

A life now left to thirst in memory

Captive to the infrequent quenching that evaporation brings

In the moment that was us, once.

AMIDST SNOWFLAKES STILL HOPEFUL

We part

Two shadows stretched out upon the wet cobblestone

Perhaps the falling snow knows the moment best

The fleeting second when lain upon our shadow

It's a star for a moment

Bright beneath the streetlight

A temporary life

Turned sour and passing down into the cracks

Left to gutter way trickles

Reflecting of the black mascara washing down upon your face

And we turn-

Two shadows outstretched and parting amidst snowflakes still hopeful.

VIRGA

The rain fingers its way across the desolate earth below

Bored and uncommitted

Like a tongue just above the skin lingering, indecisive

To the landscape below

To the seed left to wither in the cracked soil

Dry and bitter but still dreaming

Despite its earthen tomb

But such are our souls, and their love affairs with *"almost"*.

WHAT IS ART? THE ARTIST

Art is a tearing of the soul

The right words never found

A brush stroke still misplaced

That one last chisel mark breaking the stone...

And we drown,

For the mind never reveals of what our vision had truly wanted.

WRITE ME

Write me;

But only when you can crush my soul with your thoughts

Write me;

But only when you can tear my heart out with your words

Write me;

But only when you are all but desolation

Lost and adrift

Crashing

Buried

Drowned out and forgotten

Then;

Then,

We can love

Then

We can rage

Then

We can lust

In there. and only then

We just might fall upon the lie of love.

CHEAP GIN & CIGARETTES

My heart is the crushed embers of a final cigarette
Your face, just another faceless reflection in a glass of cheap gin
Some selfie in the pub each night wanting, for who knows
Caus' it's all just words written on empty pages exalting love
Marred by the ink of hopeful typeset iconography
Words formed to tell the masses something of us
Cheap gin and cigarettes.

And I count the embers as they go out one-by-one
Still hopeful in their dying.

THE HUSTLE

Cigarette smoke drifts in an intricate ballet

Caught in the glamor of a lone spotlight

Above the green stage

Below, the cue ball breaks a thousand propositions

Delicate hands assertive upon the stick

Exhaling

As skull ringed knuckles take another sip

Flat whiskey

Stale beer

Five grand cash

Balls gliding this way and that

Silently determined in their math

One pocket

Two pockets

Three

The eight-ball corner pocket called

Catching the image of a gold plated forty-five

As it rolls

The ash of a cigarette glows bright on the inhale

Black leather jacket and a wife beater shirt

Tarnished ruby red nails

A little girl smile that betrays "tough as nails"

Silence falls

The color's gone missing

Just seven stripes and a stack of Benjamin's remain

Soon, to be an already fading memory passing from the window of the 3-Train

Manhattan, Bronx, Brooklyn, Queens

"Hit the Island tomorrow", lay in her thoughts

As the city lights pass blurry, fast and hot

And a man in a hoodie say; "Bitch! Give me what you got!"

And she smiled her little girl smile

Caus' The Hustle never stops.

BAREFOOT UPON IMMORTAL LEAVES

She walks barefoot upon immortal leaves

Where a garden long lay dead

And the waterlily pond fell stagnant and drained

Below, where concrete-cast fountain Cherubs can still be found in orgy

Though their wine had run dry some time ago

And above in shadow, the Willows weep

Amidst Cottonwood snow seeds falling like sleepy stars

Gateway branches inviting of a walk upon the stone bridge

Where the moon reflects only regret

And roses withered of thirst one-by-one

Until only plastic death wreaths remained

Nylon dyed flowers fading in the sun

Fine plastic silk woven, but fraying also

Comforted momentarily in the feel of gentle footsteps, barefooted and brazen

For what is time to immortal petals,

Immortal leaves?

But for what time will take of them also.

THE STORM AMIDST A SUNNY DAY

I met an artist on the beach

Painting torrid seas upon calm sands beneath blue skies and a pleasant sun

Her brush strokes were bold and diving

The bristles of her brush rough and grinding

Urgently blending blues descending into greys then black

While above the storm clouds rolled bristling, thundering, ominous

And titanium white lightening cut its way upon the canvas stark and bright striking at a great ship below

Half drowning

Red in parts, magenta-brown in others

Its sails desperate to the stormy winds

But set to make landfall none the less

And I knew then, her heart.

MAYBE NEXT TIME

The frogs are out!
Emerged from their long winters slumber in some deep place unknown to us,
Unknown as it's always been and will be upon all our passing
Their song; the song of eons echoing
The sound of the hopeless back and forth
"If not this time, then maybe, next time..."
And they sing on amidst the babbling brook,
And I drink my Rye
And smoke my cigar
And think:
"Yeah, maybe next time." as they.

HOW HEAVY IS THE PEN

How heavy is the pen

Its poison ink

An unspoken incantation

Long undead

Set to a hopeful poem

A memory

Fallen short in death

Upon unwilling parchment

Hapless sigils

Naked upon the white

A numberless page

In an unknown book

Long locked away.

So, how heavy is the pen?

No more heavy than the heart that wields it.

THE GARDENER'S RAKE

We write

Our heart

Some word to persuade

Ourselves

Or, someone else

To leave a mark

Of any kind

But the words fall away anyways

To the ground

As deaf as the leaf

Upon indifferent grass

To wither and catch

Upon the rose thorn

Helpless to the gardener's rake

And somewhere in a trashcan

Scribbled pages meet

One last message

Before the closing of the lid

Profound and foretelling

Seen somewhere once

But still, left unread.

"WILLST SIE NOCH EINE ZIGARETTE?"

We sat in silence

Each to our plight

Each to our better days

Each a shadow in the smoke of a cigarette

Uninterested

But somehow still wanting more of it

A dart upon the board

But always fallen short

An ashtray tells a better story of love, I think

Polished nails and a Lucky Strike

A bitter Marlene Dietrich smile drenched in gin

"Willst Sie noch eine Zigarette?

(A war had wage here once, this bar, was the only thing left standing)

"Nein Baby, lass uns einfach nach Hause gehen."

MAYBE… (IN ANOTHER DRINK OR TWO)

Here…
Just waiting for the words to come
Maybe in another drink or two
Should I smoke this cigar to the nub?
What might I say
That they never heard before.
Here…
Lost in the dark
But, aren't we all?
A stubborn pen and an unwilling page
A lightless desk
And a trashcan full of half sentences.
Here…
Just waiting for the words to come
Maybe in a drink or two
Maybe in a word or two
Maybe in a smoke or two
Maybe…well, just maybe...
As we all are

Just *maybes*…

BRICK BY BRICK...

Eyes meet

Soldiers from the other side

Guards of ideology cast upon the wire

A black and white scene

Where color had once roared

Now just ashes

A city of bones where the victor's still feed

The only banner left which spoke of freedom

Was that of tiny, mismatched cloth strips hanging where

people's clothes got snatched up upon the barbed coils

Beneath the searchlights

And blood-stained buttons remind any whom might dare

A cigarette is exchanged

A temporary moment where they thought none would see

A touch of hands

Warm and reassuring

That love might still flourish beyond that place

Perhaps in some new future, soon

And along the line it came

Brick by brick

Captive to the fate of ideologies

Towering and ominous

A red knife cutting

Crushing down all hope, again

And in the grey of falling snows

And poised rifle scopes

His smile disappears from his

Brick by brick

Any hope slowly erased from them

Brick by brick

A sound of a faltering heartbeat

Brick upon brick

Two minds already trying to remember the other

Brick by brick

Lucky Strikes upon cold parched lips

Brick by brick

Soon left to be nothing, but two old photos still wishing in times echo falling

Brick by brick.

FALL IN BERLIN

The leaves lay gentle upon the cobblestone

Yellow, gold, and red

Indifferent to the ashes of a city in ruin

To the bodies heaped in unmarked graves

To the bombers overhead

To any victor

To any defeated

To any who did not listen to the poets

And here we are, again

Fall in Berlin

Indifferent leaves

Falling hapless

Expectant that the winds will take them away from here

But it doesn't

Instead,

Just the old familiar bed of cobblestone

Cold and damp

Set above the bones of yesteryear

Where the leaves fall indifferent as they always have and always will

Berlin.

UNTIL THE NEXT *"Hello"*

I wish to kiss a stranger

Any will do

In some moment upon the Seine

In a moment over spilled coffee in the rain

Let's throw in a red umbrella

And a bottle of fine champaign.

And after a day of lustful wondering

Hand in hand searching through unknown streets

A lunch under the tower

Where poets and artist still conspire to set the world ablaze in their want

We'll fall upon white linen sheets

And fuck the afternoon away.

And I think I live to hear them say goodbye

Under a lone light above a front door

"My true love comes home tomorrow,

you are a first- and last-time thing."

A careful smile fading behind a closing door

And the light above, turned off.

And I'll wish to wonder on I know

Somewhere new, far away, and best unknown

Where goodbye smiles become my fondest thoughts

What if phantoms of a restless heart

Etched and unlikely to fade

Well, at least until the next *"Hello."*

MY VAMPYR

December is nearing

The trees stripped bare

The leaves have fallen

The flowers in their winter sleep

The world falls to grey

The only color

Is you upon the stair

Beneath the world of Bruno Hass

In the footsteps of Elisa Mars

That image in my mind as I fall to sleep each night

The only thing that matters

The scene of you descending

And me waiting

Hand in hand again

Outside the cobblestone awaits

Our footsteps the laughter of our ages

Moonlight shadows stretch shy with memories

Where we will rule cities again

Immortal

For the trees will leaf in spring

And the rose is only an imitation of death

Caught red handed in its lie.

And you descend each night

My hand meeting yours

Forever, lovers

Ruling over our winters

Over lives once thought lost

Then found again

Roaming through the summer's wheat blooming

Two ghosts forever chasing leaves in the wind

Despite our faces ever fading from the mirror

But not of the other

Content in our timeless drifting

As we smile openly in our lie

Can you hear us laughing in the winds

Can you hear us telling you our truth

Can you hear us calling to the other

Forever in our descending

Upon the stair

Forever hand in hand

Always to be in that final meeting

You and I

my ЯYꟼMAV.

WE'LL KNOW THE OTHER IN THE END

Outside the rain falls torrential

The stars have all gone home

Was it seven days or seven nights?

We lost count

Outside the garden lay beaten and withered

The roses all drowned

Maybe this is it

The last moment

Our final destruction

The fireplace stages the final scene

Frame by flickering frame

Though only the window knew who the actors truly were

Your kiss gentle upon my lips

Upon my skin

Etching our last "goodbye"

Your breath

Measured and reassuring

My fist gathers up tight, warm linen sheets

The end is coming

Our hearts breaking

Sorrow for a lost future

But our souls seem indifferent

For what is hopelessness to a moment?

And the lighting tears across the sky, jagged upon our bodies

A one last polaroid moment

A one last photo of who we weren't

What will we date it

What will they say of it

What will they know of it…

That you were I, and I was you in the end.

ONE LAST CHANCE, BUT IT AIN'T ANYWHERE 'ROUND HERE

Gonna' leave you now girl

Streetside, where I found you

Here's a couple of bucks to float ya'

A hug, a kiss, and a handshake

You were the best, for the moment

Never thought we'd get here like this

But it is what it is, baby

Best to just up and walk away

Don't you think?

Caus' this John's all dried up

And your pimp don't know your value

So much for the dream

It's not that I don't love you

Just, we're all used

Two junkies under a streetlight

One for cash, the other for pleasure

Both, just barely making it

Both, just hoping to make it big, some day

Maybe in a movie, where we play ourselves

The whore and the hooker

Dreamers, dreaming

But the dreams all over in the climax

Some wet spot, on cheap hotel room sheets

Gone unwashed for weeks

A momentary gratification left wanting

Yeah, best to call it quits

End the agony

While we're ahead

See you on the other side if we survive, babe

Maybe under some streetlight in Paris

Maybe under a gas lamp in Greece, or anywhere far from here

Lovers of the impossible

Finding their chance at last

Yeah, I like that;

Lovers in their last chance,

But it ain't anywhere round' here.

WHERE THE WILDERNESS LAY UNTAMED

Petals of a flower fall

Floating aimless in the stream below

Little boats

Fleeing from the fire above

An all-consuming rage

Smoke and the flutter of bird's wings

The grass withers

Clawing boney and white as fingers from the grave

And the deer run, trampling

Leaping over unmoved bodies

Naked amongst the destruction

For what is fire to any

In a place where the wilderness lay untamed.

The Author

Brian Dennis Hartford is a published author and writer of fiction, romance, and poetry. He has a bachelor's degree in security management and has worked in the private security industry for over twenty years. He currently resides somewhere in the European Countryside.

A Special Thanks

To my wife, family, and friends and any who made this all possible. To Germany, to Europe, who has welcomed us home with open arms.

Cover Photo Source Credits

unsplash.com

Free Photos for everyone

License

All photos published on Unsplash can be used for free. You can use them for commercial and noncommercial purposes. You do not need to ask permission from or provide credit to the photographer or Unsplash, although it is appreciated when possible.

More precisely, Unsplash grants you an irrevocable, nonexclusive, worldwide copyright license to download, copy, modify, distribute, perform, and use photos from Unsplash for free, including for commercial purposes, without permission from or attributing the photographer or Unsplash. This license does not include the right to compile photos from Unsplash to replicate a similar or competing service.

Accredited Artist for photos used in cover artwork:
Photo: Valentin-Beauvais 4YrVF0gVdjk-unsplash

www.ingramcontent.com/pod-product-compliance
Lightning Source LLC
Chambersburg PA
CBHW032134090426
42743CB00007B/590